I SPY

4 PICTURE RIDDLE BOOKS

I Spy Funny Teeth
I Spy a Dinosaur's Eye
I Spy a School Bus
I Spy a Scary Monster

Riddles by **Jean Marzollo**

Photographs by **Walter Wick**

SCHOLASTIC INC. **Cartwheel** ·B·O·O·K·S·®
New York   Toronto   London   Auckland   Sydney
Mexico City   New Delhi   Hong Kong   Buenos Aires

For Chalupa,
with great thanks to Dan
—J.M.

For Elizabeth Helt
—W.W.

I Spy Funny Teeth (0-439-52472-5); Text copyright © 2003 by Jean Marzollo. "Toy Chest," "Make Believe," "Odds & Ends," and "Cubbies" from *I Spy* © 1992 by Walter Wick; "Peanuts and Popcorn" and "The Laughing Clown" from *I Spy Fun House* © 1993 by Walter Wick; "A Whale of a Tale" and "The Hidden Clue" from *I Spy Mystery* © 1993 by Walter Wick; "Yikes" from *I Spy Fantasy* © 1994 by Walter Wick; "Mapping" from *I Spy School Days* © 1995 by Walter Wick.

I Spy a Dinosaur's Eye (0-439-52471-7); Text copyright © 2003 by Jean Marzollo. "Tiny Toys," "Odds & Ends," "Toy Chest," and "At the Beach" from *I Spy* © 1992 by Walter Wick; "The Toy Box Solution" and "The Hidden Clue" from *I Spy Mystery* © 1993 by Walter Wick; "City Blocks" from *I Spy Fantasy* © 1994 by Walter Wick; "Patterns and Paint" from *I Spy School Days* © 1995 by Walter Wick; "A Secret Cupboard" from *I Spy Spooky Night* © 1996 by Walter Wick.

I Spy a School Bus (0-439-52473-3); Text copyright © 2003 by Jean Marzollo. "Tiny Toys," "Odds & Ends," "Bulletin Board," from *I Spy* © 1992 by Walter Wick; "The Mysterious Monster" and "A Whale of a Tale" from *I Spy Mystery* © 1993 by Walter Wick; "City Blocks" and "Yikes!" from *I Spy Fantasy* © 1994 by Walter Wick; "Mapping" from *I Spy School Days* © 1995 by Walter Wick.

I Spy a Scary Monster (0-439-68054-9); Text copyright © 2004 by Jean Marzollo. "Arts & Crafts" from *I Spy* © 1992 by Walter Wick; "Carnival Warehouse" from *I Spy Fun House* © 1993 by Walter Wick; "Masquerade" from *I Spy Mystery* © 1993 by Walter Wick; "Monster Workshop" and "Sand Castle" from *I Spy Fantasy* © 1994 by Walter Wick; "Storybook Theater" from *I Spy School Days* © 1995 by Walter Wick; "A Blazing Fire," "The Fountain," and "Ghost of the Night" from *I Spy Spooky Night* © 1996 by Walter Wick.

ISBN 0-439-76309-6

12 11 10 9 8 7 6 5 4 3 2   6 7 8 9 10/0
Printed in Singapore 46 • This compilation edition first printing, June 2005

I SPY

FUNNY TEETH

Riddles by Jean Marzollo
Photographs by Walter Wick

I spy

a car,

a kazoo,

a horn,

a number game,

and a box of popcorn.

I spy

a tank,

  two baseballs,

a clock,

 a frog in a truck,

and a blue wooden block.

I spy

a guitar,

a fish,

a bow tie,

a face,

an axe,

and a butterfly.

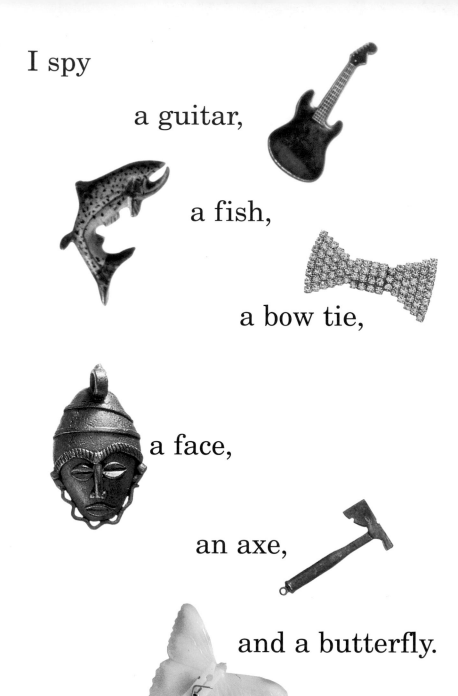

I spy

sunglasses,

a mask that's dark blue,

a clock,

a fan,

and a pink purse, too.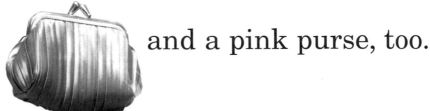

I spy

a green star,

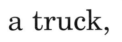 an apron that's white,

 a truck,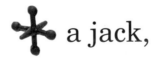

a jack,

and a red flashlight.

I spy

two gas pumps,

 a maze,

a bear,

four pink flowers,

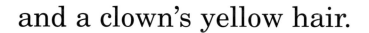

and a clown's yellow hair.

I spy

a spoon,

 a basket of fruit,

two birds,

 an S,

and a cowboy boot.

I spy

a giraffe,

 a marble,

 a king,

two googly eyes,

 and a blue-stone ring.

I spy

a domino,

 a big yellow Y,

funny white teeth,

 and a red bow tie.

I spy

five hats,

 three M's,

an E,

 a musical note,

and a zebra Z.

I spy two matching words.

red bow tie

fish

ball

red flashlight

I spy two matching words.

guitar

blue block

bus

blue mask

I spy two words that start
with the letter B.

 butterfly

face

 bear

horn

I spy three words that start with the letter P.

two gas pumps

 boot

pink purse

 truck

I spy two words that end
with the letter S.

teeth

two googly eyes

car

two birds

I spy two words that end with the letters CK.

jack

game

zebra

truck

I spy two words that rhyme.

yellow Y

 bee on a car

clock

 green star

I spy two words that rhyme.

 basket of fruit

note

 cowboy boot

sunglasses

For Ziggy, with extra thanks to Dan
—J.M.

To Abigail Helt
—W.W.

I SPY

A DINOSAUR'S EYE

Riddles by Jean Marzollo
Photographs by Walter Wick

I spy

a ball,

a bear,

a B,

and a very small

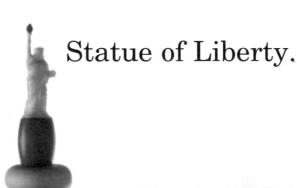

Statue of Liberty.

I spy

a palm tree,

a drumstick,

a 2,

a jar of red paint,

and a cow that can moo.

I spy

an angel,

 a dragon,

 a Q,

an egg split in half,

and a hat that is blue.

I spy

a green light,

 two blocks,

a 2,

 an old toy ship,

and a 4 of bones, too.

I spy

a magnet,

 a metal key,

a boat,

 a barrette,

an M,  and a V.

I spy

a surfboard,

a rake,

a sail,

the letter A,

and a frog in a pail.

a caboose,

a dinosaur's eye,

a large yellow e,

and a plane that can fly.

I spy

a bulldozer,

a golf ball,

a hoe,

a rope to jump,

and a man who can throw.

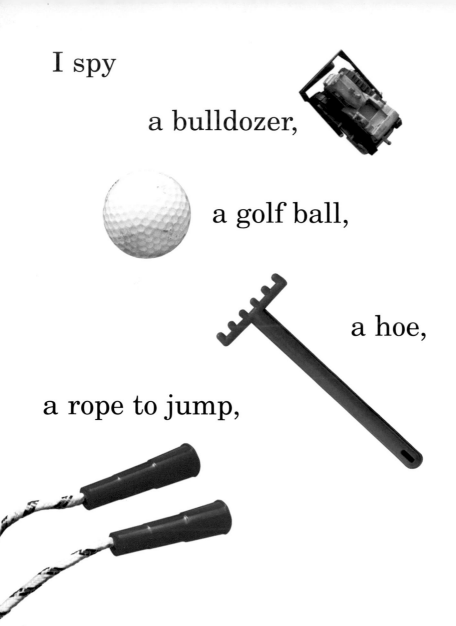

I spy

a rubber band

a bite,

 a J,

a deputy's badge,

 and the letter A.

I spy

a top,

a small saxophone,

 a large yellow eye,

and a horse all alone.

I spy two matching words.

small saxophone

 ball

very small Statue of Liberty

I spy two matching words.

plane that can fly

bear

man who can throw

I spy two words that start with the letters DR.

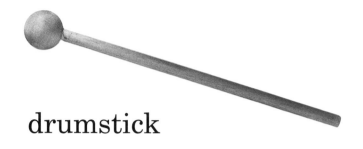

drumstick

palm tree

dragon

I spy two words that start with the letter H.

hat that is blue

angel

horse all alone

I spy three words that end with the letter T.

 green light

 magnet

 boat

 ball

I spy two words that end with the letter P.

top

bear

old toy ship

I spy two words that rhyme.

palm tree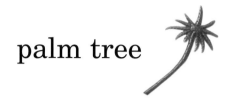

 metal key

drumstick

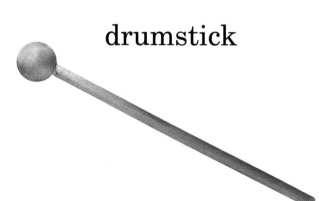

I spy two words that rhyme.

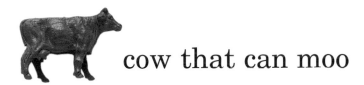 cow that can moo

boat

hat

For Karin and Sam Rees,
with thanks to Dan
— J.M.

For Melanie Word
— W.W.

I SPY

A SCHOOL BUS

Riddles by Jean Marzollo
Photographs by Walter Wick

I spy

a bus,

  two trees,

a green star,

 a hopscotch game,

and a smile on a car.

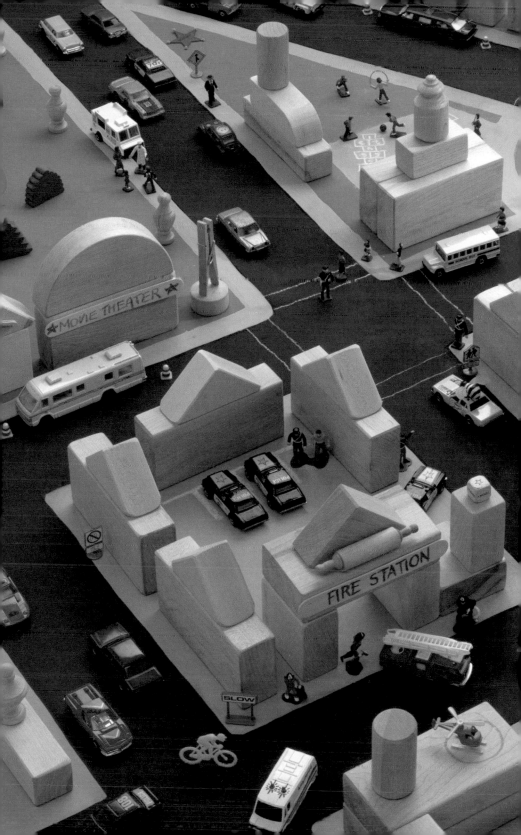

I spy

glasses

 a lobster,

five fish,

 a chick in a boat,

 and a penny for a wish.

I spy

corn,

a surfer,

a pipe,

a pink stingray,

and a car with a stripe.

I spy

a screwdriver,

 a face that's small,

scissors,

a comb,

 and a little football.

I spy 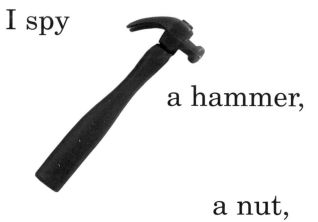 a hammer,

a nut,

 a deer,

two little stars,

 and a glass
that is clear.

I spy

a green hat,

 a boxing glove,

a duck,

and a rainbow
high above.

I spy

 five cards,

a button that's red,

 a ring,

a badge,

 and a crown for a head.

I spy

an eggbeater,

 a blue bowling pin,

a yellow fire hydrant,

and an orange tail fin.

I spy

a timer,

 a frog,

 an E,

a yellow bus,

 and a wooden D.

I spy

a bike,

 a car with a 9,

an 8,

and a truck
with MILK
on a sign.

I spy two matching words.

yellow fire
hydrant

 yellow bus

green star

I spy two matching words.

 face that's small

button that's red

pink stingray

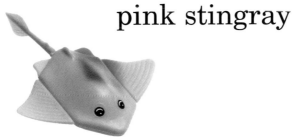

I spy two words that start with the letter C.

 corn

five cards

pipe

I spy two words that start
with the letters GL.

boxing glove

glasses

scissors

I spy two words that end with the letter N.

 orange tail fin

blue bowling pin

 football

I spy two words that end with the letters ER.

eggbeater

hammer

nut

I spy two words that rhyme.

duck

 truck

hat

I spy two words that rhyme.

 car with a 9

green star

 badge

For Peter and his cousin Dan
—J.M.

For Jack Griffin
—W.W.

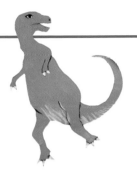

I SPY

A SCARY MONSTER

Riddles by Jean Marzollo
Photographs by Walter Wick

I spy

two paint jars,

snaky blue hair,

two horns,

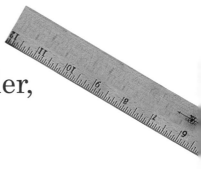

a ruler,

 and a little black bear.

I spy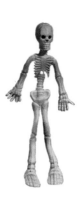

a skeleton,

 a set for tea,

 two fish,

a ship,

and a leaf from a tree.

a witch,

 a fancy chair,

 a monster tree,

and orange hair.

I spy

a crossbow,

a shield white and red,

 two small flags,

and a sand-dragon's head.

I spy

a black cat,

 a green crocodile,

a ladder,

a pail,

and a lion's smile.

I spy

a tiger,

two D's,

three O's,

a colorful pencil,

and T-Rex's toes.

I spy

a red eye,

 a spider,

 a spoon,

a spooky turtle monster,

 and a bright full moon.

I spy

a paintbrush,

two yellow laces,

a little green gear,

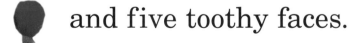
and five toothy faces.

I spy

a cork,

 a shoe that's blue,

  two bears,

two dogs,

 and a pudgy pig, too.

I spy

a fork,

a dinosaur,

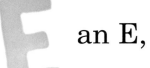 an E,

a frog,

and a ghost that's looking at me!

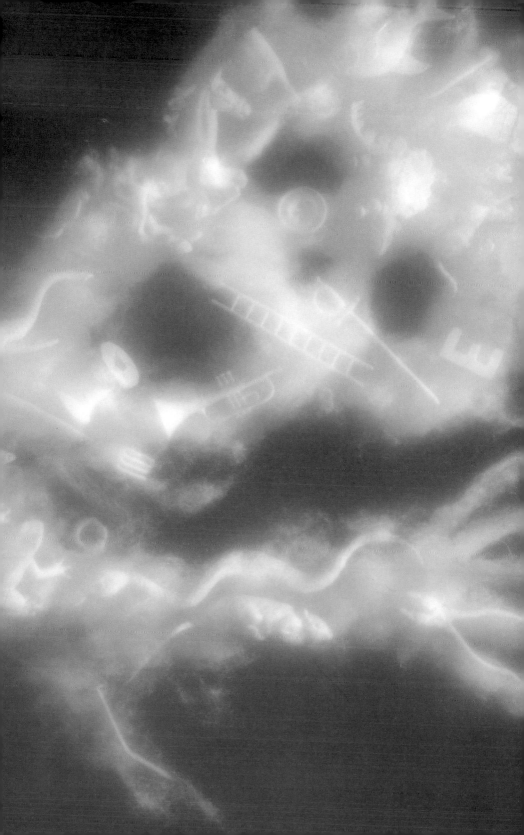

I spy two matching words.

two paint jars

a set for tea

two dogs

I spy two matching words.

a ship

little green gear

 little black bear

I spy two words that start
with the letter M.

spooky
turtle monster

orange hair

bright full moon

I spy two words that start
with the letters CR.

two small flags

crocodile

crossbow

I spy two words that end
with a silent letter E.

a toothy face

a ladder

lion's smile

I spy two words that end with the letters SH.

pail

two fish

paintbrush

I spy two words that rhyme.

fork

spoon

cork

I spy two words that rhyme.

a dinosaur

shield white and red

bright full moon